LIVING IN HISTORY

Written by Fiona MacKeith

Illustrated by Robin Edmonds
and John Cooper

HENDERSON
PUBLISHING LTD
©1997 HENDERSON PUBLISHING LTD

Time Detectives

Here's your chance to become a time traveller. Zoom through the centuries and find out about the very first people...or perhaps you would prefer to see medieval life through the eyes of a knight's visor. You can even discover how North American *shamans* (medicine men) treated illness.

People who study remains from the past, called *archaeologists*, have been able to piece together tiny fragments to give us marvellous insights into the places, peoples and lifestyles of vanished times. Here are some examples to whet your appetite.

A Real Giant

Barnum Brown, fossil collector, discovered the fossilized bones of a dinosaur in Montana, USA, in 1902. He spent three years *excavating* them (digging them up) and the beastie became known as Tyrannosaurus rex, or T. rex for short!

Model of T. rex

Bog People

The amazingly preserved remains of humans have been found in peat bogs. They may either have been the victims of sacrifices or muggings. The people who dig up the remains have to be careful not to crush or damage the delicate bodies.

Well-preserved body from Northern European peat bog

A Right Royal Cemetery

In Ancient Egypt, the *pharaohs* (kings) had enormous pyramids built to house their bodies in the *afterlife* (life after death). The pyramids at Giza have been around for over 4,500 years.

What a Way to Go

When the volcano Vesuvius, in Italy, erupted on 24 August, 79 AD, thousands of people were covered in volcanic ash and mud. This cooled, forming a solid rock case around the bodies. Although the bodies decayed, they left perfect moulds of the people's shapes.

Plaster poured in hollow reveals dead person's shape

LIVING IN HISTORY

Early People

About ten million years ago in Africa, early apes were adapting to their ever changing surroundings. Many scientists believe that these apes developed into early humans over a period of several million years.

Hello Granny!

In 1974, in Ethiopia, Africa, the fossil skeleton of an early *australopithecine* was found. That incredibly long word means that she (it was a female) could walk upright and had a bigger brain than her ape-like ancestors. Scientists named her Lucy and think that she is between one and four million years old.

Model of Lucy

Neanderthal people

Neanderthals

Neanderthal people were probably the first to wear clothes. They cared for the disabled, buried their dead and may have had a religion, too. Not bad for 150,000 years ago!

TREASURES IN DEATH

Ancient people have always treated their dead with respect. When the simple grave of a young girl was excavated in the Holy Land, she was found buried with her animal-shaped feeding bottle.

BELIEVE IT OR NOT...
During the Bronze Age, they had a very nasty little habit of beheading human sacrifices at funerals. Yuck!

DEAD SEA SCROLLS

In 1947, in a place called Qumran, a shepherd boy nipped into a local cave for a bit of peace and quiet. What a surprise when he made the historic discovery of the ancient Hebrew manuscripts now called the *Dead Sea Scrolls*, the oldest known versions of the Bible's Old Testament.

Caves where Dead Sea Scrolls were found

Dead Sea Scrolls were stored in pottery jars

Aztecs and Incas

The Aztecs and the Incas were important and powerful civilizations. The Aztecs were a wandering people who settled in Mexico in the 13th century. The Incas' great empire was centred on Peru.

Going to War
The Aztecs believed that their gods needed human sacrifices to keep the sun in motion, so they had to go to war with their neighbours to keep up the fast food supply of human bits and pieces!

Aztec warrior figure

Chocolate
Aztecs be blessed! They gave us that unbelievably mouth-watering experience – chocolate! They made a pretty fine chocolate drink using cocoa sweetened with honey and flavoured with vanilla. Mmmm...delicious!

Believe It or Not...
You might think that your teacher can overdo the discipline from time to time, but at least they don't shave your head when you fail a test – a daily occurrence in Aztec times!

A Woman's Place
Aztec women were ahead of their time. They could own property and even get a divorce.

Inca City

The Incas built a beautiful and dramatic city called Machu Picchu on a high plain between two mountain peaks. It was a natural fortress as it was protected by steep slopes and high mountains.

The remains of Machu Picchu

Sending Messages

The Inca emperor used relay runners to carry messages. Each runner used to blow on a conch shell to let the other runners know that he was on his way. The runners covered vast distances each day.

Believe It or Not...
We may never have had the muscovy duck if it wasn't for the Incas, who domesticated them. Quack, quack!

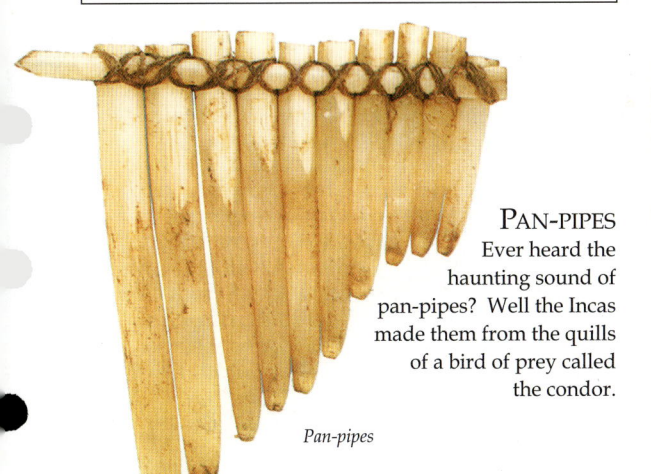

Pan-pipes

Ever heard the haunting sound of pan-pipes? Well the Incas made them from the quills of a bird of prey called the condor.

Pan-pipes

LIVING IN HISTORY 7

THE ANCIENT GREEKS

The civilization of Ancient Greece was made up of mainland Greece and many small islands scattered in the Aegean and Adriatic Seas.

Greek drinking cup

The Greeks were brilliant in the areas of literature, the arts, politics and sport, to name a few.

POWER TO THE PEOPLE
In early times, rich landowners called *tyrants* controlled the poor, until the poor took control and gained power and freedom. This new form of government was called *democracy.*

GREEK DRAMA
The Greeks were very fond of watching plays, but did you know that all the actors were male, some taking female parts? Women were probably not allowed to go to the theatre at all!

Olympic Games

The most important Greek athletics festival was held at Olympia every four years – the Olympic Games. Wars were sometimes suspended to allow people to travel to and from the Games in safety. The Olympics are still held today.

A Famous Tale

A famous Greek poet called Homer told the tale of how the Greek army captured the city of Troy.

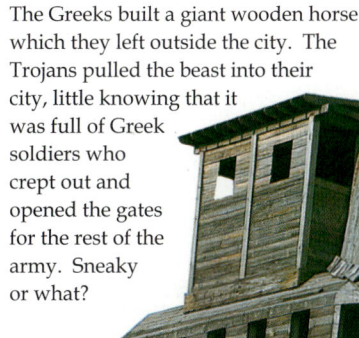

The Greeks built a giant wooden horse which they left outside the city. The Trojans pulled the beast into their city, little knowing that it was full of Greek soldiers who crept out and opened the gates for the rest of the army. Sneaky or what?

Modern replica of Trojan horse

Greek Gods

The Ancient Greeks worshipped lots of different gods and goddesses, who they thought were a lot like humans: they fell in love, married, argued and had children, to mention just a few similarities.

Zeus

Home Sweet Home
Mount Olympus, the highest mountain in Greece, was thought to be the home of the gods.

Zeus
Zeus was the king of the gods. He is usually shown as a man of great power and dignity. He sometimes carries a thunderbolt, his symbol.

Dionysos
Dionysos was the god of wine, fruitfulness and vegetation.

Apollo
The god Apollo is linked with the sun, with light, with healing and medicine. He was the brother of Artemis, the goddess of the hunt.

Aphrodite

The goddess of love and beauty, Aphrodite, was born from the sea foam. Although she was married to Hephaistos (the lame god), she fell in love with Ares, the god of war.

Aphrodite

Athena

The goddess of wisdom and warfare was called Athena. She watched over the arts, literature and philosophy.

Demeter and Persephone

This mother and daughter team were goddesses of the grain.

Greek Temples

Religion was the most important thing in Greek life, so it isn't surprising that the temples were the biggest and most beautiful buildings of all. They were made of limestone or marble, with wooden roofs and ceilings.

Temple of the Parthenon, dedicated to Athena

LIFE IN ANCIENT ROME

So legend has it, Rome was founded by twin brothers, Romulus and Remus, in 753 BC. Unfortunately, the brothers had a dreadful quarrel and Remus died... so Rome it was, after Romulus!

In legend, the infant twins were abandoned, but a she-wolf saved them by suckling them.

Coins depicting Roman emperors:

Caligula 37-41 AD

Claudius 41-54 AD

Nero 54-68 AD

HEADS YOU LOSE

The Romans didn't have newspapers or TV, so coins were used to advertise the emperor and his deeds. All the power seems to have been a bit much for some of them. Caligula went mad and was murdered, and Nero couldn't take the strain either; he went mad and killed himself!

12 LIVING IN HISTORY

The Colosseum

Inside the Colosseum

The Romans were mighty good builders. Just look at the Colosseum, the greatest of all *amphitheatres* (big buildings used for entertainment and sport). It held about 50,000 people, all of which could get out in three minutes through the 80 *vomitora* (exits).

Outside the Colosseum

Blood and Guts

There was plenty of gory entertainment to be had at the amphitheatre. The spectators enjoyed watching wild animals attacking defenceless criminals.

At around midday, all the dead bodies were removed and fresh sand was spread around, ready for a nice fresh start with the arrival of the gladiators in the afternoon. The gladiators fought each other to the death.

LIVING IN HISTORY

MORE ROMAN LIFE

Here are some down-to-earth facts about ordinary life in everyday Rome for you to devour.

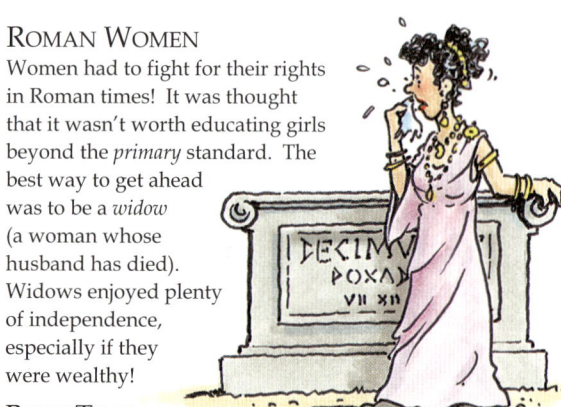

ROMAN WOMEN

Women had to fight for their rights in Roman times! It was thought that it wasn't worth educating girls beyond the *primary* standard. The best way to get ahead was to be a *widow* (a woman whose husband has died). Widows enjoyed plenty of independence, especially if they were wealthy!

BATH TIME

Most families didn't have bathroom facilities, so they went to the huge public baths instead. These weren't just places for getting clean. The men went after a day at work to exercise, chat, play games and meet friends. The women had separate baths, or they went in the morning.

Roman baths at Bath, England

Oil flask

Strigil – for scraping skin clean

KEEPING CLEAN
Forget the soap – the Romans rubbed oil all over themselves and then scraped off the sweat, dirt and oil in one go.

ROMAN TOILETS
Going to the public toilets could be quite a social event for the Romans, as they used multi-seater loos! Instead of toilet paper, they used sponges on sticks! A water channel under the seats carried the sewage away.

Roman multi-seater toilet

ANCIENT WRITING
Throughout the Roman Empire, Latin was the language which was used for all-important dealings and business. The Romans introduced the Latin alphabet to northern Europe and it is still used there today.

LIVING IN HISTORY

THE ANCIENT EGYPTIANS

The Ancient Egyptian civilization lasted for many centuries, from about 3,000-300 BC. The Egyptians were well-known for their amazing pyramid-building skills, but here are some other facts that you may not be so familiar with.

JUST TAKING A NAP

Before the Egyptians became experts in *mummification* (preserving bodies), they arranged a dead body in a sleeping position and buried it in sand. This absorbed all the water from the body and preserved it. Then the person's spirit could recognize it and inhabit it again in the afterlife. Very handy!

Preserved body of a 5,000-year-old man

STORAGE JARS

Once the Egyptians developed the art of mummifying bodies, there was no stopping them. Even beloved pets and other creatures were mummified. The mummy's vital organs had to be removed, dried out and then stored in jars.

Canopic jars – for storing organs in

Tutankhamun

Tutankhamun is probably the most famous pharaoh. He was laid to rest with a solid gold mask weighing over 10.2 kg (22.5 lb). Myth has it that he laid a curse on all who entered his tomb.

A Gritty Problem

There was nothing that the Egyptians liked better than a good party. Eating could have been a little tricky for some Egyptians, though. Grit got into the flour when the bread was made and this wore their teeth away. Ouch!

Tutankhamun's mummy mask

Looking Good

The Egyptians wore wigs made from human hair and stuck them in place with beeswax. Some tied cones of scented animal fat to their wigs! In the words of one top ten Egyptian hit song, 'Put myrrh on your head and dress up in beautiful clothes'!

Courtiers with cones of animal fat on their head

The Vikings

Vikings were brave warriors and explorers from Norway, Sweden and Denmark. For 300 years, from the 8th to the 11th centuries, they took the world by storm with their daring raids.

Where They Went
Thanks to the Vikings' excellent seafaring skills and their sensational ships, they could take other people completely by surprise. The brown parts on this map show where the Vikings had settlements.

Viking Attire
Viking warriors didn't wear uniforms. Each soldier had to supply his own clothes and weapons. The more important Vikings got to wear iron helmets, while the poorer ones had to make do with leather caps. Not ideal in a battle situation!

Iron helmet

18 LIVING IN HISTORY

Home Life

Vikings who made it to Iceland had to make do with the building materials that they found. Because timber was scarce, the walls and roofs of the houses were often made from turf. Wood panelling helped to keep out the cold and damp.

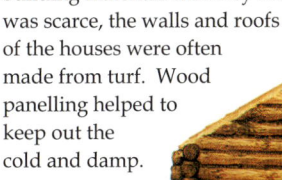

End view of Viking house with turf roof

That's It Folks!

When it came to dying, the Vikings didn't believe in leaving anything to chance and were buried with everything they would need in the next world. The wealthiest were buried in boats crammed full of belongings. Even servants were killed and sent off to the next world with their masters! The ships were then often set alight in a blazing *funeral pyre*, or covered with mounds of earth.

Re-enactment of a Viking funeral pyre

MEDIEVAL LIFE

Medieval times were also called the *Middle Ages*. This was roughly the time between the 5th century to the end of the 15th century...so that's quite a bit of history!

REVOLTING PEASANTS
Medieval peasants had a tough time. After a lethal plague called the *Black Death* wiped out thousands of people, the survivors in England had to work extra hard and pay extra taxes. They got fed up with this and in 1381 they marched to London, led by a chap called Wat Tyler, to complain to the king about their treatment.

Rat – plague spreader

WHAT A STINK!
Peasants didn't wash their outer clothes. It's a good job that they kept big fires going because the woodsmoke acted as a deodorant and kept the pong down a bit!

BREATH FRESHENER
Medieval toothpaste was made from ingredients such as ground up oyster and whelk shells. And if you had a touch of bad breath, well you just sweetened it with honey, coriander and cumin seeds. Simple!

LIVING IN HISTORY

Farming

In medieval Europe, more than 90 per cent of the population lived and worked on the land. They often used a *three field system* where two fields were sown with crops in one year and the third field was left to recover, so it would be good for growing things the next year. If a harvest failed, it could mean that a whole village starved.

Stained glass shows farmer sowing seeds

Indoor Loo

By the late 15th century, many houses had the luxury of an indoor loo. It wasn't much to write home about, as it was only a closet in the wall with a hole over a cesspit. There would probably have been an outside loo, too.

The 'smallest room'

LIVING IN HISTORY 21

LIFE IN A CASTLE

A castle was a private fortress, owned by a nobleman or a baron. It was also a home and a community with lots of staff to look after the day-to-day running of the place.

ENEMIES BEWARE

Castles were incredibly strong buildings with walls as thick as 4 m (13 ft). Marauding enemies were always a danger. They sometimes tried to tunnel under the walls, but bowls of water put on the ground were a good early warning, as the vibrations made the water ripple.

If you think that's sneaky, what about *murder holes!* These holes in the roof could be used to rain down scalding water, hot sand or other horrible bits and pieces on the heads of the intruders.

Food Glorious Food

The main hall was where people ate, slept and carried out business. Breakfast consisted of bread soaked in ale or watered-down wine. The main meal was eaten at about ten or eleven o'clock in the morning. Then there were various suppers in the evening.

An Early Start

When as young as seven years old, a boy from a noble family might be sent to a castle to become a *page* and learn good manners. Girls were often sent to a castle to learn the arts of sewing, home-making and how to behave correctly, especially in front of the gentlemen.

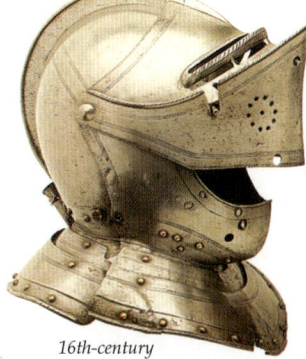

16th-century knight's helmet

Fit for Fighting

Lords were also knights. They could be called to fight for their king at any time. Taking part in *tournaments,* where they entered team games or single combat, kept them in practice.

Believe It or Not...

Pigs were bred for the meat that they provided, but they were also trained as retrievers, like modern dogs. They were used when poaching!

LIVING IN HISTORY

KNIGHTS

Who were knights? They were warriors who fought on horseback and date back to 800 AD. When we talk about knights today, we probably mean the 11th-century knights in armour.

SUITS OF ARMOUR

Early armour was made from *chain mail* and was easy to slip on over the head. But a suit of armour was a weighty business. By the time all the gear was in place, it could weigh up to 25 kg (55 lbs) and was pretty hot!

Getting kitted out

Fully dressed

BEST BEHAVIOUR

When knights weren't fighting, they traditionally behaved in a courteous way and they had their own knightly code of conduct. It placed special emphasis on showing excellent manners towards women. Knights who displayed these qualities were known as *chivalrous*.

LIVING IN HISTORY

Jousting

It must have been a scary sight to see a knight charging towards you on horseback! The knight's aim was to shove his opponent off his horse with a single blow of his *lance*. Jousting required special armour, but it was so heavy that the knight could hardly move in it!

Mrs Knight

A knight's lady was expected to run the castle's domestic affairs and have children. When a knight married, all his wife's goods became his, so knights were often on the lookout for a rich partner!

Japanese armour

Japanese Knights

Japan had its own kind of knight called a *samurai*. A samurai had to be prepared to fight to the death for his supreme lord, called the *overlord*. In samurai families, Japanese women were sometimes trained to fight as well.

Farming

Farming began more than 10,000 years ago in Turkey and the Middle East. People discovered that certain grasses had seeds which could be eaten and also planted to grow new crops.

Grinding Grain

Early farmers ground their grain into flour. They did this with a *stone quern* (hand mill) which was simple to use but must have been very time consuming. The grain was placed on the flat surface, then the lump of stone was used to grind the grain down.

Farming Towns

Farming made a lot of wealth. Towns with hundreds of houses were built and most of the people worked on the land, growing cereals and fruits and raising livestock. Other people made clothes, pottery and tools which they traded with farmers for food.

Part of an early Turkish town – most of its people farmed

Harvest

Everyone helped to gather in the crops. The women, children and men all worked together to cut the wheat with *sickles,* being careful not to shake loose any of the precious grain. Then the wheat was tied into bundles and taken to the barn once it had ripened. Finally, the whole harvest was *threshed* (beaten) to loosen the grains.

Tithes

Villagers had to give the priest a tenth, or a *tithe,* of everything that they produced – anything from crops to eggs! This made the church very wealthy.

Animal Power

Animals have been used to pull ploughs since early times. Even camels and llamas have been used in some countries.

In 18th-century Europe, horses became the main method of pulling new farm machinery, such as ploughs. This century, tractors have taken their place, although poorer countries still use animal power.

Horses at work

Modern tractor

Sailing

People the world over have always wanted to explore and claim new lands. In the earliest days, one way to get there was by boat.

Egyptian Ideas
The Egyptians thought that the world was flat and that the heavens were supported by four massive pillars. However, when Egyptian sailors were sent out by Queen Hatshepsut in 1490 BC and reached as far as the Indian Ocean, the Egyptian priests said that the supports were further away than they thought!

Around the World
Ferdinand Magellan is said to have been the first to sail around the world. Well, his ship might have, but he didn't! Only one of his five ships returned after the gruelling three-year voyage, and Magellan was not on board!

Ferdinand Magellan

Believe It or Not...
In 1492, Christopher Columbus discovered America. The only thing was, he set off in search of China!

Hard Tack
Sailors often spent many months away from home. They lived in cramped, dirty conditions. After the first few days, the fresh fruit and vegetables ran out and they had to live on *hard tack* – horrible rock-hard biscuits which often became infested with maggots.

Rats
Very often, a ship's *hold* (where the cargo is stored) was infested with rats. The fleas that lived on the rats were responsible for spreading the *Black Death*, or *bubonic plague*, which reached Europe in the mid-14th century. It killed about one-third of the total European population.

Piracy
Pirates sailed the seas, attacking and robbing treasure-laden ships. They were bold brutes who showed no mercy to their victims.

Many of the crew were once-honest seamen who got fed up with the life of maggoty biscuits and rats, and joined the pirate ranks.

SOLDIERS

A soldier is trained for battle. It's an unfortunate fact of life, but there have been battles since time began!

GREEK SOLDIERS
Greek soldiers were called *hoplites*. They had to pay for their own armour and equipment, and for this reason only men from wealthy families could be hoplites.

Hoplite

BELIEVE IT OR NOT...
If you were in the French infantry during the Napoleonic period, you stood a good chance of being shot by your comrades from behind. They weren't as skilled as they might have been in loading and aiming their guns!

QUICK MARCH
Soldiers are trained to take the same sized paces so that they will all move at the same speed. To this day, a *pacing stick* is used in the British army to make sure that this happens.

MARKS OF RANK

Badges of rank make it easy to recognize another soldier's status. The North American Plains Indian used to wear an elaborate feather headdress to mark him out as a cut above the rest.

GRUB UP!

During the Crimean War (1853-56), the British soldiers were served such awful grub that a great chef, Alexis Soyer, was sent out to the battle front to try to spice things up a bit.

WOUNDS AND DEATH

During the Crimean War, the sick and wounded lay dying in the rat-infested corridors of Scutari Hospital in Turkey. But when Florence Nightingale (nicknamed *the lady with the lamp*) arrived in 1854, she soon got things shipshape and cut the death rate to 2.3 per cent within six months. Good old Florrie!

Cowboys

Cowboys were horsemen who raised and herded cattle on the plains of North and South America. Sometimes, authorities and citizens thought that these people were wild and dangerous, but they became national heroes.

Cowboy Gear

Dressed for the practical, tough, outdoor life, the cowboy had essential items of clothing and equipment.

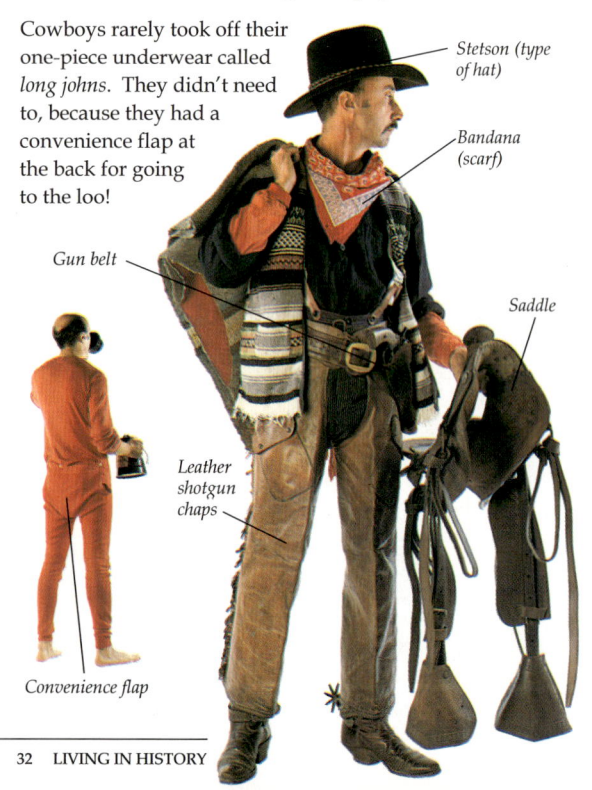

Cowboys rarely took off their one-piece underwear called *long johns*. They didn't need to, because they had a convenience flap at the back for going to the loo!

Stetson (type of hat)

Bandana (scarf)

Gun belt

Saddle

Leather shotgun chaps

Convenience flap

32 LIVING IN HISTORY

A cowboy's boots had high heels to stop them from slipping through the stirrups. They could be dug into the ground, too.

The spiky bits, called *spurs,* on the back were used to dig at the horse's sides to make it move. This wasn't as cruel as it sounds because the whole point of spurs was to penetrate the horse's thickly matted hair, so that it could feel the prod.

Spur

DIFFERENT NAMES

Cowboys had different names depending on where they came from: *gaucho* in Argentina, *llanero* in Venezuela and *huaso* in Chile. They all did the same kind of job though, and loved their independent way of life.

Gaucho's clothes

Poncho

Panuelo (knotted scarf)

Bombachas (trousers)

BELIEVE IT OR NOT...
A cowboy sat on his saddle for up to 15 hours a day! Ouch!

LIVING IN HISTORY 33

NORTH AMERICAN INDIANS

By 1500, there were more than 300 tribes of North American Indians. Large numbers lived east of the Mississippi, in California, and in the Northwest. Their way of life centred around their hunting and artistic skills.

The Indians' world was changing all the time: they had to move around because of droughts and fighting between tribes, and the animals they hunted became extinct. Over the next 400 years, Europeans brought changes that caused the downfall of the Indian way of life.

INDIAN GEAR

The Dakota Indians were the lords of the North American plains by the mid-1800s. They terrorized their Indian enemies. Here, you can see the ceremonial dress of a Dakota elder (senior member of tribe).

Shirt made from mountain sheepskin

Eagle feather headdress

Beaded moccasins (shoes)

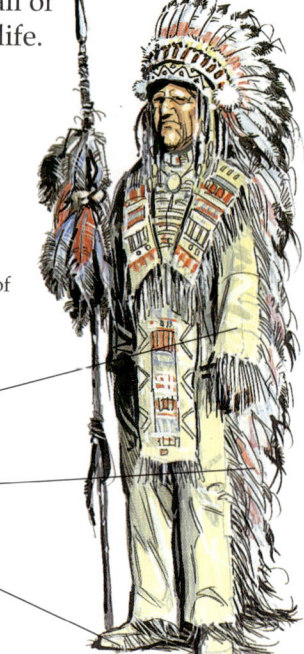

Peace-pipe

The Menominee Indians believed that smoking increased their wisdom. At important discussions or ceremonies a pipe called the *calumet* was passed around. Because these get-togethers often happened at the end of fighting, the pipe became known as the *peace-pipe*.

Sacred Menominee calumet

The Family Home

The *tipi* was the traditional Indian family home. It was made from a cone of long poles covered with buffalo hides and decorated with traditional painted designs. There was space inside for a family, their bedding and their belongings.

Tipi

Invasion

When white settlers arrived, things began to go badly for the Indians. The settlers brought diseases which the Indians couldn't fight against, they claimed all the richest land and broke agreements about land ownership. The free-roaming Indians were herded on to *reservations* – areas of land set aside where they had to live.

Cars, Boats and Planes

Where would we be without transport? Sitting at home, probably! Here are just a few fascinating facts about historical ways of getting about.

The Automobile

The *automobile,* or car, was invented in 1885 when the *Benz Velo* went on sale to the public. It had a top speed of 20 mph (32 kph)! Built at the pioneering factories of Karl Benz in Germany, it was the first car to sell in large numbers.

Benz Velo

Henry Ford

Car maker Henry Ford could be said to have put America on the road. By 1930, over 15 million of his Model T Fords had been made on his car assembly lines and sold.

Model T Ford

Balloons and Airships

The first people who successfully took to the skies went up in a hot-air balloon in 1783.

By the 1920s, enormous airships were ferrying people across the Atlantic Ocean. Tragedy struck one called the Hindenburg in 1937, when it went up in flames.

The Wright Brothers

In December 1903, the inventor brothers Orville and Wilbur Wright took to the air in their powered plane. It flew unsteadily for 40 m (131 ft) and then came down to land safely. This was a historic first powered flight.

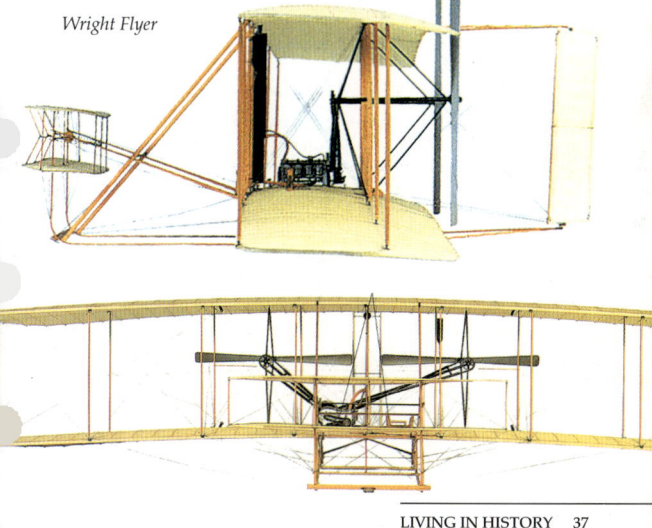

Wright Flyer

LIVING IN HISTORY 37

DAFT INVENTIONS

Through the ages, those clever inventor people have come up with some pretty nifty bits and pieces to change our lives, but some have been a little on the odd side!

What, No Hands!

In the early days of motoring, long before indicators were invented, a weird and wonderful cable-operated hand device was developed which clipped on to the car door. It was operated from a knob on the dashboard, so that the driver could give hand signals. It even lit up at night!

Cable-operated hand

Warm Toes

John Logie Baird might have given us television (which he did in 1934), but try as he might, he couldn't get his self-warming socks to work!

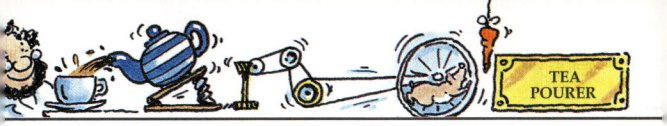

A Stitch in Time
Isaac Singer built the first sewing machine in 1889.

Food Fact
The tin opener wasn't invented until 44 years after the arrival of tinned food! Handy!

Fast Flush
A kind of flushing toilet was being used by the rich way back in 1596, but toilet paper wasn't invented until 1857. Hmmm!

Before the Bike
Before the bicycle, people used a machine called a *hobby horse* to get around. Constructed of a wooden beam over two spoked wheels, the rider sat on the plank and pushed the ground with their feet...and went very slowly. Uh oh!

Filling the Cavities
For those of you with a thing about the dentist, the first dental drill was a clockwork wind-up affair which kept going for a full two minutes. Agony!

Harrington's clockwork dental drill

LIVING IN HISTORY

RELIGION

There are literally hundreds and hundreds of religions around the world. Some go back thousands of years while others are modern-day. Here are one or two facts about a very few of them.

CHRISTIANITY

Christians believe that Jesus Christ is the Son of God. Their symbol of the cross stands for the cross on which Jesus was crucified. Christianity began in Jerusalem, in Israel. Today, there are over 20,000 different branches of Christianity because of disagreements over ways to practise the faith.

A dove – symbolizes the Holy Spirit

The cross – symbol of the Christian religion

BUDDHISM

The Buddhist faith began in India. Today, it has spread throughout most of Southeast Asia. It is based on the teachings of an Indian prince who lived a life of meditation and preaching and became known as Buddha.

The symbol of Buddhism is an eight-spoked wheel.

ISLAM

The Islamic faith is based on belief in one God – Allah – and it began in Mecca, in Saudi Arabia. People who follow Islam are called Muslims. The religion is based on the teachings of the prophet Muhammad, Allah's main messenger.

The Muslim's symbol is a star and a crescent moon.

JUDAISM

Followers of Judaism are called Jews. Judaism began in the *Promised Land*, in Israel. The Jews believe in one God, who revealed the Law to his people. Their symbol is the Star of David.

This case shows the Star of David. A tiny parchment scroll with biblical texts is enclosed.

HINDUISM

Most Hindus believe in many gods, but they all believe that when a person dies their soul is reborn again in another body. Hinduism began in India and is spread throughout much of Southeast Asia. Their symbol is a sacred sound, OM.

SIKHISM

Sikhism is based on the worship of one God and on the cycle of rebirth. It began in north India and today has spread to Britain and North America. Its symbol is a design of weapons.

Sikh symbol – steel ring, a two-edged sword and crossed, curved swords

LIVING IN HISTORY

Clothes

Clothes have been worn for many thousands of years. The first people made clothes to protect themselves from the cold, the heat and the rain. Since those early times, clothes have become much more than basic essentials; they are fashion items.

A Cover-up
In the *Renaissance* (14th-17th centuries), the man about town was a very fashionable sight in his *doublet*. He wore a *codpiece* over his well...his more intimate bits! Often highly decorated, it used to cover up the flap opening in his tights!

Wigs Galore
During the 18th century, wealthy men and women wore extremely tall, white powdered wigs. The only trouble was that they ran the risk of being set alight by chandelier candles!

NAME TAPES

The Ancient Egyptians were the first to use name tapes. As all their linen clothes looked the same, they needed a way to identify what belonged to whom.

STEEL HOOPS

In 1856, ladies probably gave a huge sigh of relief. Instead of wearing up to six petticoats to achieve the perfect figure, they used a flexible frame called a *crinoline*. It was made of steel hoops and either one or two petticoats could be slipped over the top.

Crinoline

ALL GATHERED IN

Since time began, women have been pulled, padded and lifted, but there can have been little worse than the rigid, immovable *corsets* of the 1880s which caused fainting attacks, broken ribs and displaced organs!

LIVING IN HISTORY

MEDICINE

From earliest times, plants and herbs have been used as medicines. Prehistoric people used *catmint* for colds and *rue* for headaches, whilst the Incas used *urine* (wee) for treating fever! Since then, there have been many developments in the field of medicine.

MEDICINE MEN
The native North American *shaman* was a man or woman believed to be able to harness the supernatural forces of the spirit world. Shamans used dramatic ceremonies to help sick people reject their illness by mind power.

FALSE TEETH
The first well-fitting false teeth were made in 1774. They had springs to keep them in place!

Wooden wand held by shaman during healing ceremony

Coiled spring

Porcelain teeth

Surgery

Before the 1800s, surgery was very often more threatening than the problem which needed treating! Luckily, the 19th century saw the discovery of new surgical equipment, *anaesthetics* and *antiseptics*. This was a far cry from the Middle Ages when surgery was often performed by barbers! Uh oh!

Steel surgical instruments could stand high-temperature sterilization.

Penicillin

In 1928, British scientist Alexander Fleming discovered the bacteria-killing properties of a substance made by a mould (fungus) called Penicillium. He called his discovery penicillin, and millions of people worldwide owe their lives to it.

New Limbs

Replacement limbs were made in the 17th century. The artificial hand shown here was made of iron.

17th-century iron hand

LIVING IN HISTORY 45

Food

Nowadays, foods from different countries are available in other parts of the world, but it hasn't always been that way. At one time, you could only get food from the place where you lived. Explorers and traders helped to take new foods to the countries that they visited and this livened up the local diets no end!

Believe It or Not...

A delicacy that the Romans couldn't resist was dormouse cooked in honey and poppy seed!

Bog Man's Stomach

The 2,000-year-old body of a man was found preserved in a peat bog near Grauballe, Denmark. His stomach revealed millions of intestinal worms' eggs which would have lived in poorly-cooked meat, so we know that he was a meat-eater. His tum also contained his last meal – vegetable soup and muesli. Yuck!

The body found near Grauballe

VIKING MEALS

Viking settlers on the Atlantic islands enjoyed poached gulls' eggs. The gulls didn't do much better though, as they got roasted as a quick snack! Roast horse was also on the menu. The Vikings stewed their meat in huge pots, or *cauldrons*, made of iron. In times of famine, the Vikings sometimes killed their old people and children so they wouldn't have to feed them!

Viking cauldron

PIRATES AHOY

When pirates could get it, they usually lived on turtle meat. If shipwrecked or stuck in calm seas they were even known to eat their satchels! They left the recipe:

> Slice the leather into pieces, then soak and beat and rub between stones to tenderise. Scrape off the hair, and roast or grill. Cut into small pieces and serve with lots of water.

TABLE MANNERS

During medieval times, an aspiring young lord might be given a few table tips which included: don't remove your hat as lice will drop into the grub...and don't pick your nose! Well!

LIVING IN HISTORY 47

INDEX

Africa 4
amphitheatres 13
apes 4
archaeologists 2
armour 23, 24, 25
Aztecs 6

Baird, John Logie 38
baths 14
Benz, Karl 36
bicycles 39
Black Death 20, 29
Bronze Age 5
Brown, Barnum 2

cars 36, 38
castles 22, 23, 25
church 27
clothes 4, 20, 26, 32, 33, 34, 42-43
Columbus, Christopher 28
cowboys 32-33
Crimean War 31

Dead Sea Scrolls 5
dentistry 39, 44
dinosaurs 2

Egyptians, Ancient 3, 16-17, 28
Europe 15, 21, 27, 29, 34

farming 21, 26-27
Fleming, Alexander 45
food 23, 26, 27, 29, 39, 46-47
Ford, Henry 36

gods/goddesses, Greek 10-11
Greeks, Ancient 8-9, 10, 11, 30

Homer 9
hygiene 14, 15, 20, 21, 39

Incas 6, 7
Indians 31, 34-35
inventions 38-39

jousting 25

knights 2, 23, 24-25

Magellan, Ferdinand 28
medicine 2, 44-45
medieval (Middle Ages) 2, 20-21, 47
mummies 16, 17

Neanderthal people 4

Olympic Games 9

religions 4, 11, 40-41
Rome, Ancient 12-15, 46

samurai 25
seas 8, 18, 28, 29, 47
shamans 2, 44
soldiers 9, 18, 30-31

television 38
tithes 27
Tutankhamun 17

Vikings 18-19, 47
volcanoes 3

wigs 17, 42
Wright, Orville and Wilbur 37

Acknowledgements: American Museum of Natural History, New York; Barleylands Farm Museum; British Museum; Graham High, Centaur Studios (model-makers); Museum of Mankind; National Maritime Museum, Greenwich, London; Norfolk Rural Life Museum; Pitt Rivers Museum; Science Museum, London; University of Trondheim, Norway; Viking Ship Museum, Oslo, Norway; Walsall Leather Museum; Weald and Downland Open Air Museum.

Picture Credits: (KEY: a=above, b=bottom/below, c=centre, l=left, r=right, t=top) Ancient Art & Architecture Collection: 14; 25b; Bruce Coleman Ltd: 40cl; DAS Photo: 19b; Forhistorisk Museum, Moesgard: 46; Sonia Halliday Photographs: 17tr; 17b; Michael Holford: 1; 11tl; Hutchison Library: 5b; INAH: 6cr; Simon James: 13tr; 15br; Jewish Museum, London: 41t; Scala: 10; 12t; Syndication International: 28br; Trip/Helene Rogers: 41bl; Universitets Oldsaksamling, Oslo: 18; Worthing Museum & Art Gallery: front cover bc; Zefa/Neville Presho: 7tl; /Konrad Helbig: 11b.

Additional Photography: Peter Anderson, Jane Burton, Geoff Brightling, Andy Crawford, Geoff Dann, Mike Dunning, David Exton, Lynton Gardiner, Christi Graham, Dave King, Richard Leeney, John Lepine, Liz McAulay, Nick Nichols, James Stevenson, Clive Streeter.

Models: John Denslow, Andrew Nash.

Every effort has been made to trace the copyright holders. Henderson Publishing Ltd apologises for any unintentional omissions and would be pleased, in such cases, to add an acknowledgement in further editions.